broom

crab

frog

Say the name of the picture.
Write the 2-letter blend you hear at the beginning.

Name _____

 Cut out the pictures. Paste them in the right places.

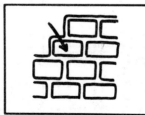

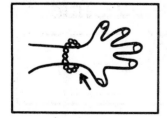

White

Name _____

Write the 2-letter blend **br**, **cr** or **fr**.

 __own

 __ead

 __ack

 __uit

 __og

 __oss

 __own

 __y

 __ame

 __anch

 __oom

 __ayon

 __ush

 __ick

Name _____

 tr

 dr

 gr pr

Say the name of the picture. Write the 2-letter blend you hear at the beginning.

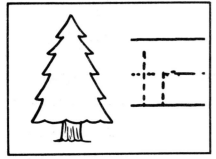 tr

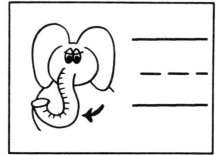 _ _ _ _

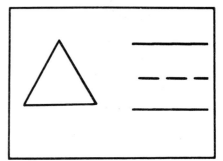 _ _ _ _

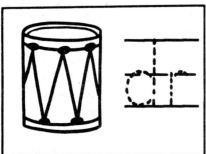 dr

 _ _ _ _

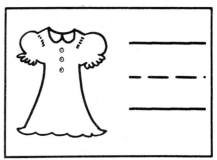 _ _ _ _

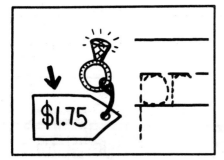 pr

 _ _ _ _

 _ _ _ _

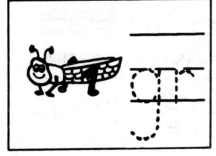 gr

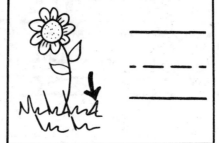 _ _ _ _

 _ _ _ _

4

Name _____ Skill: Consonant blends tr, dr, gr, pr

Write the 2-letter blend **tr**, **dr**, **gr** or **pr**.

__uck

__agon

__ice

__um

__ill

__isoner

__ize

__ee

__ass

__ess

__in

__unk

__apes

__ain

FS-2656 Phonics Workbook-Blends & Digraphs

Name _____

Color the pictures that begin like 🌲 **tr** and 🐛 **gr** blue.

Color the pictures that begin like 🥁 **dr** and 🐸 **fr** yellow.

Name _____

gr

pr

br

tr

dr

fr

cr

Say the name of the picture.
Write the 2-letter blend you hear
at the beginning.

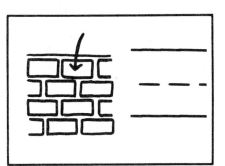

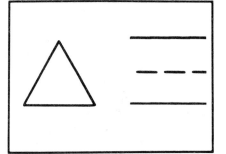

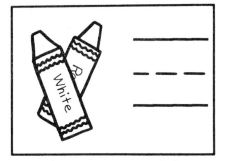

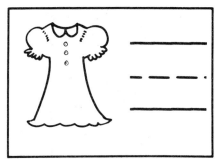

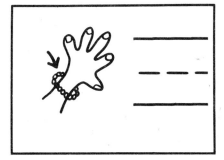

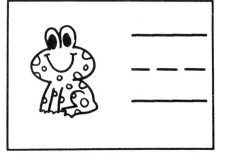

Cut out the pictures. Paste them in the right places.

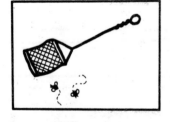   

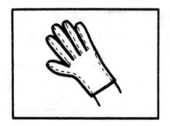   

Name _____

cl cl

clown

fl fl

flower

Say the name of the picture.
Write the 2-letter blend you hear at the beginning.

FS-2656 Phonics Workbook-Blends & Digraphs

Write the 2-letter blend **cl**, **fl** or **bl**.

__aw

__y

__am

__ock

__ag

__imp

__oud

__ame

__ock

__ack

__ower

__ouse

__ow

Grandma's House

__own

10

Skill: Consonant blends bl, gl, pl

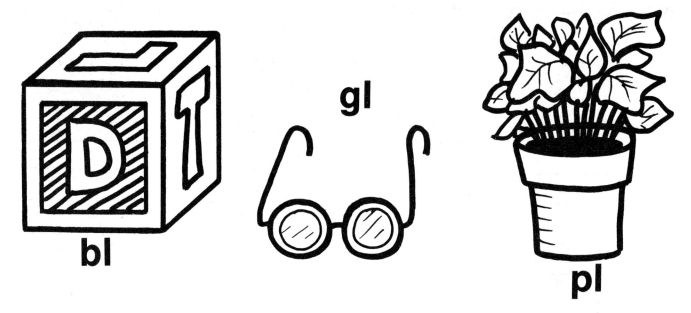

gl

bl

pl

Say the name of the picture. Write the 2-letter blend you hear at the beginning.

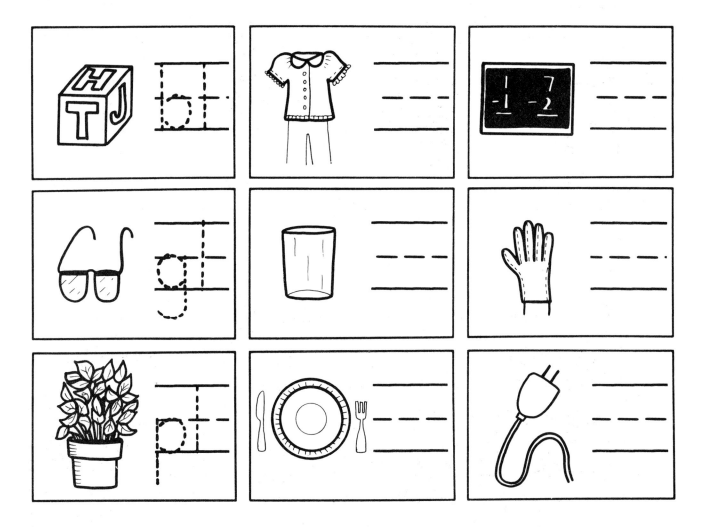

Write the 2-letter blend **bl**, **gl**, **pl** or **cl**.

 __ __ove

 __ __ate

 __ __ane

 __ __ock

 __ __ass

 __ __ue

 __ __ow

 __ __imp

 __ __ug

 __ __asses

 __ __am

 __ __ouse

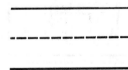 __ __obe

 __ __ant

Name _____

Color the pictures that begin like

 cl and   pl blue.

Color the pictures that begin like

 bl and   fl orange.

FS-2656 Phonics Workbook-Blends & Digraphs

Name _____ Review: L blends

Say the name of the picture. Write the
2-letter blend you hear at the beginning.

gl
bl
fl
pl
cl

 _ _ _ _ _

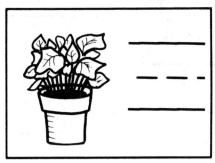 _ _ _ _ _

 _ _ _ _ _

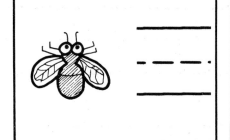 _ _ _ _ _

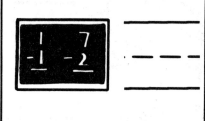 _ _ _ _ _

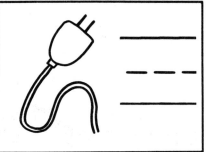 _ _ _ _ _

 _ _ _ _ _

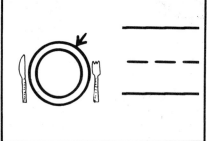 _ _ _ _ _

 _ _ _ _ _

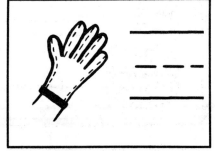 _ _ _ _ _

 _ _ _ _ _

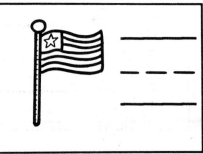 _ _ _ _ _

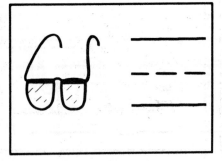 _ _ _ _ _

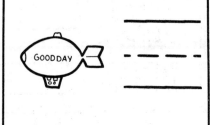 _ _ _ _ _

 _ _ _ _ _

FS-2656 Phonics Workbook-Blends & Digraphs

st st

star

sn sn

snake

Say the name of the picture. Write the 2-letter blend you hear at the beginning.

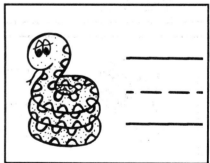

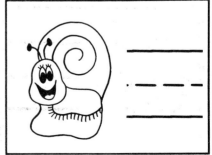

Cut out the pictures.
Paste them in the
right places.

 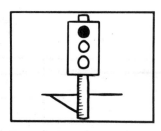  

 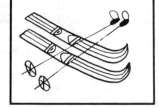  

Name _____

sl

sc

sw

Say the name of the picture. Write the 2-letter blend you hear at the beginning.

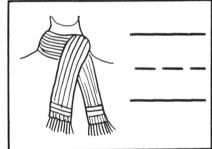

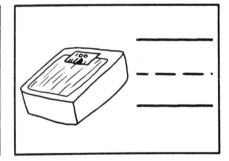

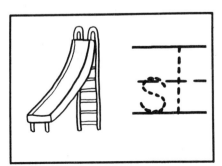

Name _____

Write the 2-letter blend **st**, **sn**, **sl** or **sc**.

__ __amp

__ __ale

__ __ory

__ __ed

__ __op

__ __ide

__ __owman

__ __ool

__ __eeve

__ __ail

__ __ork

__ __arf

__ __ake

__ __ar

Name _____   Skill: Consonant blends sc, sw, sp, sn

Write the 2-letter blend **sc**, **sw**, **sp** or **sn**.

__ill
_____
_____

__ale
_____
_____

__oon
_____
_____

__ot
_____
_____

__owman
_____
_____

__ing
_____
_____

__ider
_____
_____

__ail
_____
_____

__eater
_____
_____

__an
_____
_____

__ake
_____
_____

__arf
_____
_____

__ow
_____
_____

__ooter
_____
_____

FS-2656 Phonics Workbook-Blends & Digraphs

Name _____

Color the pictures that begin like and  red.
sk   **sc**

Color the pictures that begin like and  green.
sn   **sp**

sk   **sm**   **st**   **sp**

Say the name of the picture. Write the 2-letter blend you hear at the beginning.

Name _____

Write the 2-letter blend **sk**, **sm**, **st** or **sl**.

__amp

_____
- - - - - - - - -
_____

__ates

_____
- - - - - - - - -
_____

__ory

_____
- - - - - - - - -
_____

__ed

_____
- - - - - - - - -
_____

__irt

_____
- - - - - - - - -
_____

__op

_____
- - - - - - - - -
_____

__ide

_____
- - - - - - - - -
_____

__ile

_____
- - - - - - - - -
_____

__unk

_____
- - - - - - - - -
_____

__oke

_____
- - - - - - - - -
_____

__ool

_____
- - - - - - - - -
_____

__ar

_____
- - - - - - - - -
_____

__is

_____
- - - - - - - - -
_____

__eeve

_____
- - - - - - - - -
_____

Name _____

Say the name of the picture. Write the

2-letter blend you hear at the beginning.

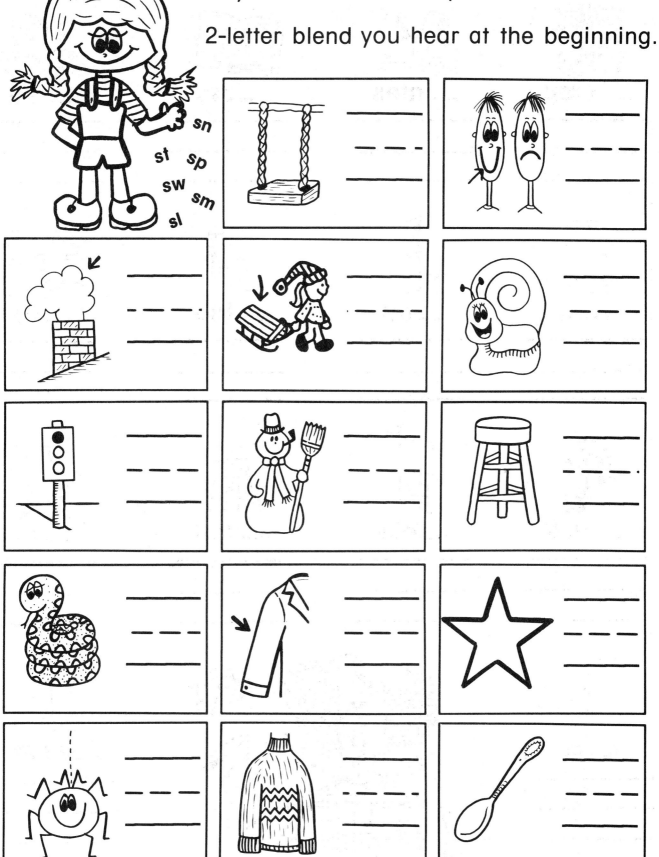

sn

st   sp

sw   sm

sl

Name _____

Circle the 2-letter blend you hear at the beginning of each word.

 **br** **fr** **gr**	 **bl** **cl** **fl**	 **sk** **sl** **sn**
 **cr** **dr** **tr**	 **cl** **fl** **gl**	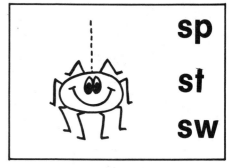 **sp** **st** **sw**
 **br** **tr** **pr**	 **fl** **gl** **pl**	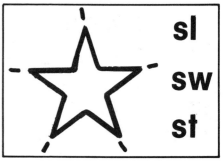 **sl** **sw** **st**
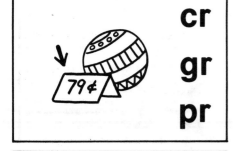 **cr** **gr** **pr**	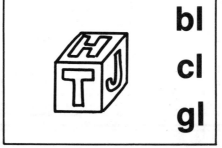 **bl** **cl** **gl**	 **sk** **sl** **sn**
 **br** **pr** **cr**	 **cl** **bl** **pl**	 **sk** **sw** **sn**

Name _____

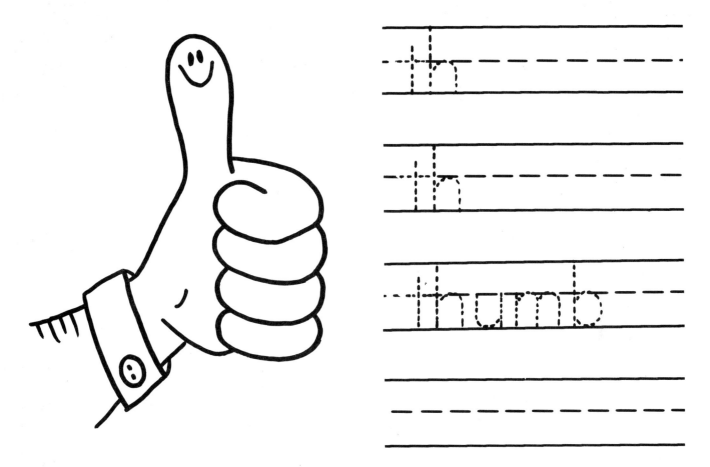

Say the name of the picture. Write the 2-letter digraph you hear at the beginning.

Name _____

Yes   Cut out the pictures.
Paste them in the
right places.   No

th	
th	
th	
th	

13   30

    FS-2656 Phonics Workbook-Blends & Digraphs

Name _____

Write the letters **th**

if the picture begins like  .

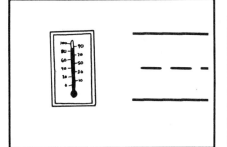

| 13 _____ |

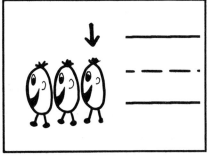

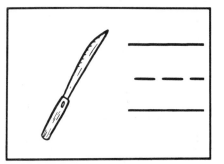

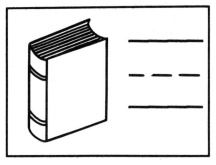

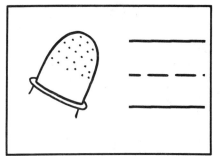

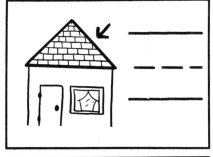

30 _____

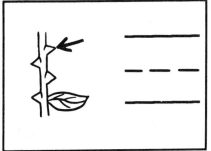

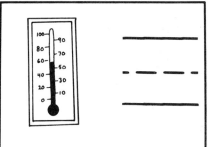

27   FS-2656 Phonics Workbook-Blends & Digraphs

wh

wh

whale

Say the name of the picture. Write the 2-letter digraph you hear at the beginning.

Write the letters **wh**

if the picture begins like .

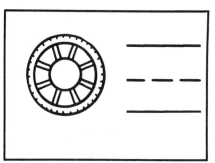

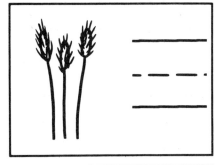

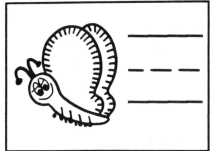

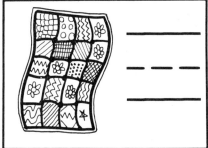

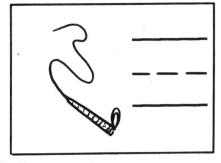

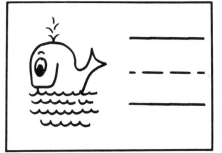

Yes

Cut out the pictures.
Paste them in the
right places.

No

wh

wh

wh

wh

FS-2656   Phonics Workbook-Blends & Digraphs

Name _____

Write the 2-letter digraph **th** or **wh**.

 __in

 __istle

 __ip

 __eel

 __iskers

 __ird

 __ite

30 __irty

 __ale

 __orn

__eat

__umb

__imble

13 __irteen

Say the name of the picture. Write the 2-letter digraph you hear at the beginning.

Name _____

Write the letters **sh**

if the picture begins like .

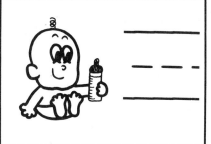

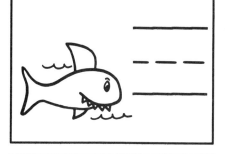

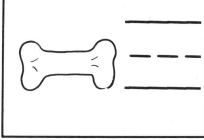

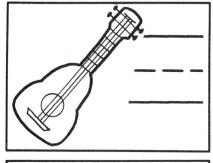

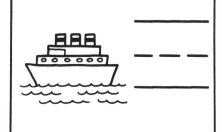

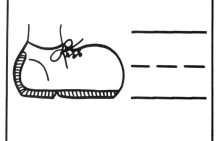

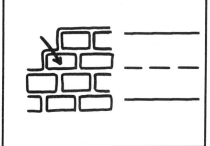

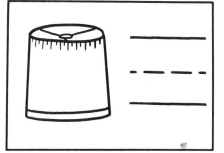

Name _____

 Yes   Cut out the pictures.
Paste them in the
right places.   No

sh		
sh		
sh		
sh		

Name _____

Write the 2-letter digraph **th** or **sh**.

__oe

_____

__ell

_____

__ip

_____

__irty

_____

__adow

_____

__eep

_____

__imble

_____

__irt

_____

__ovel

_____

__irteen

_____

__ade

_____

__orn

_____

__umb

_____

S.S. RUB A DUB...

__ird

_____

Color the pictures that begin like  th yellow.

Color the pictures that begin like  sh green.

Color the other pictures purple.

30				
	13			
			8	

 **th**

 **sh**

Say the name of the picture.
Write the 2-letter digraph you hear at the beginning.

30 ___	(ship) ___	(shark) ___
(thimble) ___	(thumb) ___	(shovel) ___
(sheep) ___	(shoe) ___	(thorn) ___
(thermometer) ___	(shell) ___	13 ___

FS-2656 Phonics Workbook-Blends & Digraphs

ch

ch

chicken

Say the name of the picture.
Write the 2-letter digraph you hear at the beginning.

FS-2656 Phonics Workbook-Blends & Digraphs

Name _____

Skill: Consonant digraph ch

Write the letters **ch**

if the picture begins like  .

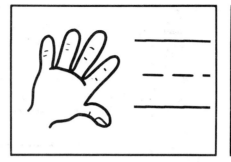

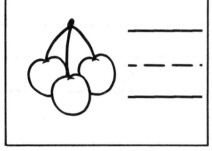
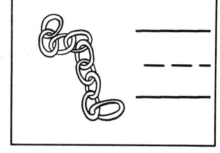

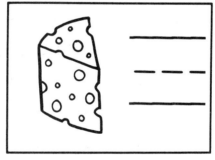

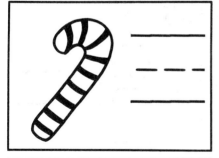

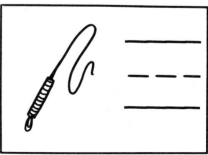

FS-2656 Phonics Workbook-Blends & Digraphs

 Yes

Cut out the pictures.
Paste them in the
right places.

 No

ch

ch

ch

ch

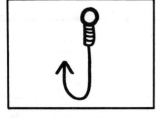
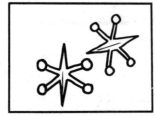
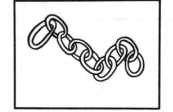

40

FS-2656   Phonics Workbook-Blends & Digraphs

Write the 2-letter digraph **ch** or **wh.**

__istle
_____
- - - - - - - - -
_____

__ain
_____
- - - - - - - - -
_____

__ip
_____
- - - - - - - - -
_____

__eel
_____
- - - - - - - - -
_____

__ale
_____
- - - - - - - - -
_____

__ite
_____
- - - - - - - - -
_____

__erries
_____
- - - - - - - - -
_____

__eese
_____
- - - - - - - - -
_____

__eat
_____
- - - - - - - - -
_____

__ick
_____
- - - - - - - - -
_____

__in
_____
- - - - - - - - -
_____

__iskers
_____
- - - - - - - - -
_____

__imney
_____
- - - - - - - - -
_____

__air
_____
- - - - - - - - -
_____

Color the pictures that begin like red.

Color the pictures that begin like  blue.

Color the other pictures yellow.

Name _____

 **ch**    **wh**

Say the name of the picture.
Write the 2-letter digraph you hear at the beginning.

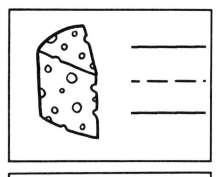 _ _ _ _ _ _ _

 _ _ _ _ _ _ _

 _ _ _ _ _ _ _

 _ _ _ _ _ _ _

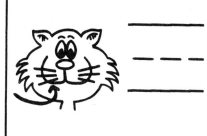 _ _ _ _ _ _ _

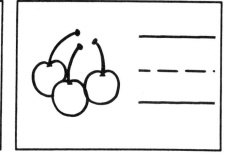 _ _ _ _ _ _ _

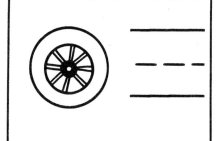 _ _ _ _ _ _ _

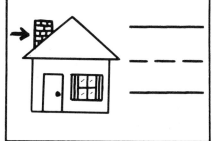 _ _ _ _ _ _ _

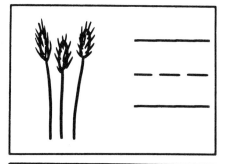 _ _ _ _ _ _ _

 _ _ _ _ _ _ _

 _ _ _ _ _ _ _

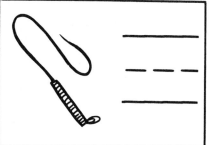 _ _ _ _ _ _ _

Name _____

Write the 2-letter digraph **sh** or **ch**.

__eep

_____
- - - - - - - -

__ild

_____
- - - - - - - -

__ick

- - - - - - - -

__ade

- - - - - - - -

__erries

_____
- - - - - - - -

__in

_____
- - - - - - - -

__adow

_____
- - - - - - - -

__imney

- - - - - - - -

__ip

_____
- - - - - - - -

__ain

_____
- - - - - - - -

__ell

_____
- - - - - - - -

__eese

_____
- - - - - - - -

__ovel

_____
- - - - - - - -

__irt

_____
- - - - - - - -

Name _____

Write the 2-letter digraph **sh**, **ch** or **wh**.

__iskers

_____
_____

__ip

_____
_____

__ovel

_____
_____

__eat

_____
_____

__oe

_____
_____

__ade

_____
_____

__ain

_____
_____

__istle

_____
_____

__imney

_____
_____

__ild

_____
_____

__adow

_____
_____

__in

_____
_____

__eese

_____
_____

__eel

_____
_____

Write the 2-letter digraph **th**, **sh** or **ch**.

__ild

_____

_____

__irteen

_____

_____

__umb

_____

_____

__ick

_____

_____

__irty

_____

_____

__oe

_____

_____

__imble

_____

_____

__ell

_____

_____

__orn

_____

_____

__eep

_____

_____

__erries

_____

_____

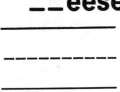
__irt

_____

_____

__eese

_____

_____

__ip

_____

_____

FS-2656   Phonics Workbook-Blends & Digraphs

__oe

 __istle

 __ip

 __imble

 __ell

 __eep

 __eel

 __erries

 __ild

 __ip

30 __irty

 __ick

 __eese

 __ale

FS-2656 Phonics Workbook-Blends & Digraphs

Name _____

Circle the 2-letter digraph you hear at the beginning of each word.

th
ch
sh
wh

th
ch
sh
wh

th
ch
sh
wh

th
ch
sh
wh

th
ch
sh
wh

th
ch
sh
wh

th
ch
sh
wh

th
ch
sh
wh

th
ch
sh
wh

th
ch
sh
wh

th
ch
sh
wh

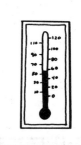

th
ch
sh
wh

th
ch
sh
wh

th
ch
sh
wh

th
ch
sh
wh

FS-2656   Phonics Workbook-Blends & Digraphs